Animal F

George Orwell

Guide written by John Mahoney

A *Letts* Literature Guide for GCSE

Contents

Plot summary

1 The animals of Manor Farm, mistreated by the farmer Mr Jones, are told of a dream by Old Major, a well-respected boar. Old Major's dream is of a time when animals will be free to control their own destinies without interference or exploitation by man.

4 Conflict occurs between Snowball and Napoleon, and it becomes obvious that Napoleon has ambitions to rule alone. The animals labour together, taking inspiration from the titanic efforts of the horse Boxer, who adopts as his motto: 'I must work harder'. They find learning very hard work and most of them give up.

2 Old Major dies, but his dream is kept alive by the pigs Napoleon and Snowball. One night, driven by anger and hunger, the animals, led by Napoleon and Snowball, rise up and drive Farmer Jones and his wife from the farm.

3 The animals rename the farm Animal Farm and create Seven Commandments by which they agree to be ruled. Snowball is active in committees and in helping to educate the animals. Napoleon takes on the education of a litter of puppies, isolating them from the other animals.

5 Jones and some neighbouring farm workers attempt to win the farm back but are beaten off. The final conflict between Napoleon and Snowball comes when the animals vote about building a windmill. Snowball is accused of betraying the revolution and Napoleon sets his 'secret police', the dogs he has been 'educating', onto Snowball, who has to flee for his life.

6 Once he has undisputed control of Animal Farm, Napoleon proves an even more brutal ruler than Farmer Jones.

8 Napoleon and his pig henchmen open up trade with the human beings and the novel ends with Napoleon and the other pigs playing cards with the local farmers in Mr Jones's farmhouse.

7 The Seven Commandments are re-written and discarded one by one. Finally, all that is left is a statement that 'All animals are equal, but some animals are more equal than others'.

9 The starving animals, looking in through the windows, are unable to distinguish the men from the pigs. Old Major's dream has turned into a nightmare.

Who's who in *Animal Farm*

Old Major

Old Major represents both Marx and Lenin in that he introduces the fundamental theories and ideals on which the revolution is to be based. One Marxist theory expressed is that an animal's labour has more intrinsic value than is required for its own needs. The surplus is stolen by parasitic man. There is irony here in the way in which Napoleon eventually steals the results of the animals' labour for his own needs. It is also ironic that, under Mr Jones's authority, the farm was less productive than it is after the revolution and that consequently there was less for Mr Jones to steal.

The 'Lenin' side of Old Major's character is shown in the part of his speech which reduces complex philosophy to fundamental propositions or maxims which everyone can understand. There is also a parallel between the homage paid to Old Major's skull by the animals and the exhibition of Lenin's embalmed body in Red Square, Moscow. However, notice that Old Major's identification with Lenin is not complete: he dies before the Rebellion, whereas Lenin led the October Revolution. In this respect, Snowball (mainly identified with Trotsky) takes on the Lenin role.

Napoleon

In many ways, Napoleon represents Joseph Stalin, the tyrannical ruler of the USSR after the Russian Revolution. However, as his name suggests, Napoleon is made up of characteristics which many dictators have shared throughout history. One criticism of this characterisation might be that Napoleon is unbelievable because he has no redeeming features. However, bearing in mind why Orwell wrote this novel, it is perhaps wrong to expect the characters to be rounded or fleshed out. The novel is a political satire or allegory, and it is a feature of such writing that events are simple and characters two-dimensional in order to put the author's message across in the most effective way.

Although Napoleon may have no redeeming features morally, he has qualities which make him stand out from the other pigs. He is described in Chapter 2 as 'a large, fierce-looking Berkshire boar with a reputation for getting his own way'. He and Snowball are described as 'pre-eminent among the pigs' before the Rebellion. Napoleon succeeds in building up support from the animals even before the machine of propaganda (Squealer and Minimus) and terror (the dogs) is in place.

Lacking the idealism of Old Major or Snowball, Napoleon is a political opportunist. His ruthlessness and determination more than make up for his lack of intellect — as is the case with many dictators.

Snowball

Looking at *Animal Farm* as an allegory of the Russian Revolution, Snowball represents Trotsky. Like Trotsky, Snowball is a brilliant speaker and is the intellectual inspiration for the revolution. He is described in Chapter 2 as 'a more vivacious pig than Napoleon, quicker in speech and more inventive'. He works sincerely and selflessly for the benefit of all the animals. Orwell makes fun of some of Snowball's behaviour, but nevertheless clearly intended Snowball to represent a hopeful alternative to Napoleon. He is not perfect, however. He is part of the group of pigs that steals the apples and the milk.

Snowball's character is a study of a <u>sincere revolutionary who is out-manoeuvred by a more ruthless and cunning opponent</u>. He becomes obsessed with the windmill and spends hours working on his designs for it. He does not realise that the other animals are not able to understand his ideas for renovating the farm or his hopes for the future. He is completely unaware of Napoleon's plans to overthrow him and he <u>runs away without a fight</u> when the inevitable happens. Snowball's <u>ideas are misappropriated</u> and his <u>character vilified by Napoleon</u> in order to deceive and betray the animals.

Squealer

Squealer is one of the four pig founders of the new society formed after the revolution. Like Napoleon, <u>he is an opportunist</u>. It is not clear how much of his <u>propaganda</u> is the work of Napoleon and the other pigs, and how much of it is his own. Squealer is presented as a small fat pig, nimble in mind and body. He thrives with the growth of the new society and achieves high status within it. He plainly enjoys his work, which is essential to Napoleon's success. At the very first mention of Squealer <u>it is said that he could 'turn black into white'</u>, and this is his job as head of Napoleon's propaganda machine. He is <u>the equivalent of the vast media machine that presented the government's version of events</u> in the USSR. All dictatorships have used a similar device.

Squealer deals in <u>half-truths, omissions and plain lies</u>. He feeds the illusions that help the workers to endure their harsh existence. His purpose is <u>to stifle public understanding or awareness of real events</u> and so forestall any challenge to the pigs' power.

Boxer

Boxer is an enormously strong horse upon whom the work of the farm, and therefore its survival, depends. He is a gentle giant and his philosophy is simple, based on the dignity of labour. He is not very intelligent and is described by Orwell in Chapter 1 as 'not of first rate intelligence, but he was universally respected for his steadiness of character and tremendous powers of work'. He is exploited by whoever runs the farm and, because of his crucial importance in the farm work and his lack of any sort of critical perception, he unwittingly contributes to the exploitation of other animals.

Boxer represents the ordinary worker: decent, honest and essential to the success of any social system. Such a worker is inevitably exploited under a dictatorship or totalitarian regime. Even after his death, Boxer's favourite slogans, 'work harder' and 'Napoleon is always right', are used cynically to control the other animals. He never realises that the ideals of the revolution are being corrupted, but at least he is spared the sight of pigs and men becoming indistinguishable in the final scenes. Boxer's experiences under the regime at Animal Farm show what can happen when the actions of those in power are accepted unquestioningly.

Benjamin

Benjamin is a cynic – one who doubts the sincerity or ability of those around him. He is also sceptical – he doubts the truth of many theories or facts. Benjamin learns to read, but he consistently refuses to put this skill to any useful purpose. Only at the final collapse of Animalism ('All animals are equal, but some are more equal than others') does Benjamin agree to read the

Commandment(s) to the animals. By then Muriel, the usual reader, is dead. Benjamin can be seen as representing the uninvolved intellectual who achieves nothing, despite his wisdom. He is also a great survivor: 'the oldest animal on the farm' in Chapter 1, and still there at the end. Do not, however, forget his loyalty to Boxer and his frantic attempts to save him.

Clover

Clover is the maternal figure of the farm. Her good sense is sound if limited, and complements Boxer's qualities of simple goodness and strength. More than any other, she is the animal who displays sympathy and kindness. She is disturbed in a way that the others are not by the outrages which take place on the farm. However, she is a survivor and is a source of comfort and strength for the oppressed animals. She, like Boxer, represents the ordinary person who is unwittingly manipulated and exploited within a dictatorship.

Dogs and sheep

The dogs and the sheep are each treated as a group, not as individuals, and each group reveals qualities traditionally associated with the animal. Dogs and sheep clearly represent two important groups in Soviet society (or any dictatorship): the secret police suppressing opposition through fear and intimidation, and the easily manipulated, slogan-chanting masses.

Mr Jones

Mr Jones is the cause of the rebellion at the farm in the same way that Czar Nicholas II was, in very simple terms, the cause of the Russian Revolution. Mr Jones has fallen on hard times, and so there is some excuse for his drunkenness, but his brutality to and neglect of the animals are less excusable. Mr Jones is the most fully developed of the human characters but is still little more than a stereotype.

Pilkington and Frederick

Pilkington and Frederick represent types of man, but also different nations. Pilkington is a gentleman farmer whose farm, Foxwood, is badly managed because he spends all his time enjoying country sports. Frederick is aggressive, efficient and extremely cruel to the animals on his farm, unlike Pilkington who is merely neglectful.

There is an obvious link between Frederick and Germany: Frederick the Great was a famous Prussian king, and 'Pinchfield' (i.e. 'steal land') is a reference to Hitler's territorial ambitions. Pilkington, therefore, must represent the Allies, particularly Britain and France – 'Foxwood' sounds British, with its suggestions of hunts in the countryside. Note the way that Napoleon sides with first one and then the other. This is the equivalent of Stalin's treaties with, in turn, Nazi Germany and the Western Allies.

About the author

George Orwell

Animal Farm, written in 1943–44 and published in 1945, is now considered by many to be George Orwell's finest novel. Although he wrote fiction successfully in the 1930s, his other outstanding novel, *Nineteen Eighty-Four*, also an attack on totalitarian regimes like the USSR, was not published until 1949. Orwell's best-known books from prior to *Animal Farm* are sociological and political non-fiction and reflect his own life and views very strongly.

Born Eric Blair in 1903, he was educated at Eton and took up a conventional colonial career with the Indian Imperial Police in Burma. He found this sort of work intolerable and left the force in 1927: his life there is charted in *Burmese Days* (1935). He returned from India with a hatred for imperialism and lived for several years in Paris and London, taking any employment he could. He was quite poor, earning modest sums as a journalist and a private tutor, taking casual jobs and attempting to run a village store. Orwell wrote two startling accounts of the life of the poor during this period: *Down and Out in Paris and London* (1933) and *The Road to Wigan Pier* (1937).

In 1936 Orwell married and, hoping to help the left-wing republican government in their fight, he and his wife moved to Spain, as did a number of other socialists from around Europe. Despite ill-health, Orwell volunteered in 1936 to fight in the Spanish Civil War against Franco's Fascists: his experiences, which included being wounded, are recounted in *Homage to Catalonia* (1938).

The Soviet Union supported the Communist opposition to Franco, and as Orwell was always a left-wing thinker and an opponent of privilege, we might expect him to take a favourable view of the Soviet Union, as many in Britain did at the time. However, he was a passionate believer in justice, freedom and equality, and far too honest to pretend that Stalin's Soviet Union encouraged these. In Spain he had joined (by mistake, as much as anything) a Trotskyite group, POUM, which the Russian-controlled Communists suppressed, though they were, in a sense, 'on the same side'. He was appalled when, in August 1939, Stalin and Hitler signed a non-aggression pact which encouraged Hitler's invasion of Poland.

By the time that Orwell came to write *Animal Farm*, the Soviet Union had joined the war against Nazi Germany and patriotic Britons were not expected to criticise our brave allies. Orwell was not surprised when his regular publisher, Victor Gollancz, refused the book. In a letter to a friend in February 1944 he wrote, 'it is so not OK politically that I don't feel certain in advance that anyone will publish it'. By the time Secker and Warburg published it in August 1945, the war was over and suspicion between the West and the USSR had returned.

Animal Farm deals with how people behave before, during and after revolutions in general, and Orwell makes general political points, but there is no doubt that he is specifically attacking the Soviet Union. In a preface to the Ukrainian edition in 1947 he wrote, 'And so for the past ten years I have been convinced that the destruction of the Soviet myth was essential if we wanted a revival of the Socialist movement'. He went on to write, 'I proceeded to analyse Marx's theory from the animals' point of view', though it was necessary in the novel to alter the exact chronology of events. The final scene with the farmers, he explained, was based on an event that was taking place as he began writing the book: the Tehran conference of 1943 between Roosevelt, Churchill and Stalin: 'I personally did not believe that such good relations would last long; and, as events have shown, I wasn't far wrong'.

George Orwell died in 1950.

Historical background

The Russian Revolution of 1917 was really two revolutions, like the animals' Rebellion and Battle of the Cowshed, although in Russia different people took part. The February Revolution was a spontaneous response to suffering and hunger (and also to Russian disasters in the First World War) and led to a moderate government. The October Revolution established the Bolsheviks (Communists) in power, with Lenin supreme and Trotsky and Stalin both prominently placed. As with the Battle of the Cowshed, the October Revolution occurred after conservative forces attempted to re-capture St Petersburg; Trotsky, like Snowball, distinguished himself by his generalship.

By the time of Lenin's death (1924), the Union of Soviet Socialist Republics (USSR) was firmly established and the leadership was the subject of a power struggle between Stalin and Trotsky (Napoleon and Snowball).

One of the major differences between the two was that Trotsky believed in the international co-operation of workers, leading to world revolution, while Stalin advocated 'socialism in one country'. This is reflected in *Animal Farm*, as are the stages by which Trotsky became a non-person (literally being air-brushed out of history by doctoring photographs) and was exiled from the Soviet Union in 1929. He was eventually murdered in Mexico in 1940.

The old Russian Empire had been largely agricultural, with a large peasant population, but the Soviet Union moved towards increasing industrialisation and vast collective farms. Orwell depicts the treatment of peasants who opposed collectivisation (joining small farms together under state control) in the episode with the hens who oppose proposals to take their eggs. In *Animal Farm*, the knoll can be seen to represent Russian feeling for the land, for Mother Russia, and the windmill represents industrialisation.

An over-simplified, but basically accurate examination of Soviet life before the Second World War reveals three further tendencies:

- The early free debates of political ideas were succeeded by a totalitarian dictatorship banning free speech: 'totalitarian' means centrally controlled by only one party.
- Industrial progress was charted in a series of Five-Year Plans, the successes of which were exaggerated, but which became more realistic and more aimed at international trade as time went on.
- Finally, all hints of opposition were ruthlessly suppressed: the secret police (OGPU) and show trials awaited Stalin's enemies.

You will find equivalents of all these in *Animal Farm*.

In the late 1930s, conflict between Nazi Germany and the West became increasingly likely. The Soviet Union attempted to play one against the other, as Napoleon does with Frederick and Pilkington. The pact between Germany and the USSR, agreed in 1939, was suddenly broken when Hitler's troops invaded Russia in 1941. The destruction of the country was savage, but, with heroic resistance, notably at the siege of Stalingrad, the Soviets forced a German retreat the following year: paralleled in the Battle of the Windmill. The Soviet Union was thus drawn into war on the side of the Western Allies.

Lenin, like Old Major, was a powerful orator.

Themes and images

Revolution and corruption

Animalism, the revolutionary doctrine adopted by the animals, is based on Old Major's teaching in the same way that Communism was originally based on the teachings of Karl Marx. However, Communism can mean different things to different people and in different societies. Specific Communist countries are as much influenced by individual leaders and particular national characteristics as they are by political doctrines.

It is a mistake to consider *Animal Farm* as a satire only on Communism. Animalism is interchangeable with a range of 'isms': fascism, socialism, conservatism, flat-earthism and so on, in that it is not so much the doctrine that is corrupt or faulty, as the individuals in power. Old Major, despite his good intentions, fails to notice a crucial point: while his ideas may be sound and his intentions high-principled, corrupt individuals will find ways to twist them to their own purposes. What happens in *Animal Farm* shows this. Corruption means moral deterioration, which is exactly what happens to Old Major's ideals once Napoleon puts them into practice.

Animal Farm plots Napoleon's corruption and his decline into most of the seven deadly sins: pride, lust, envy, gluttony, anger, laziness, and desiring others' goods. Corruption is also evident through the destruction of the Seven Commandments and the enforcement of the one Commandment: 'All animals are equal, but some animals are more equal than others'. This clearly shows how elitist the pigs have become and how the ideals of Animalism have become a thing of the past.

Communication

Throughout the story, events are rewritten according to the prevailing political needs of the pigs. This is an effective way of staving off nostalgia, or the tendency to romanticise the past. In *Animal Farm*, the pigs manage to turn nostalgia on its head by referring to the bad old days of life under Mr Jones. They make the past seem worse than it actually was in order to make their own brutal excesses seem less shocking to the animals. The control of books, of thought and of history is a vital weapon in the armoury of authoritarian political systems.

The constitution of *Animal Farm* is contained in Seven Commandments. These are slowly corrupted over the course of a few years, and their original meaning is changed. Eventually, none of Old Major's revolutionary principles are left and the remaining Commandment, which is the creation of the corrupt pigs, is simply a licence for the pigs to do as they please.

Orwell was conscious of the interaction between opinion and language. He said of *Animal Farm* that it was, 'The only one of my books I really sweated over'. He said his aim was 'to fuse political and artistic purpose into one whole'. In that sense, he was himself engaged in a kind of propaganda exercise, wanting his readers to learn from the story.

Propaganda is the spreading of a particular idea, doctrine, policy or opinion, with the intention of influencing people. How were Boxer, Clover and the other animals so deceived that they elevated Napoleon to the status of a demi-god? To achieve this, the pigs used the tools of dictatorship — the manipulation of emotions such as fear, anger and patriotism; the giving of misinformation; and the control of basic necessities like food and education — which can be used to 'persuade' individuals to take the propagandist's point of view. All Squealer's speeches are propaganda, as are Napoleon's and the poetry of Minimus. So too, though less obviously, are speeches by Moses the raven.

The power of the written word and development of mass communications mean that it is essential for any would-be dictator or power-hungry politician to gain control of the media. The failure to use one's mental capacity, by allowing others to think for you and by being, like Muriel the Goat, satisfied with the 'rubbish heap' as the main source of news, is a disservice not only to oneself but to the whole of society.

Text commentary

Chapters 1–3

Chapter 1

Animal Farm is described on the title page as '<u>a fairy story</u>'. You may well wonder why: there are no fairies in it and, though the story is not naturalistic, it evidently deals with **<u>the real world of ideas and politics</u>**. Perhaps George Orwell wanted to disarm criticism, to pretend that it was a children's book, because he encountered much opposition to the political message. Or perhaps it was just an ironic joke. There are, in fact, several terms that you should consider in relation to *Animal Farm*, and these are discussed below.

- An <u>animal fable</u> is an ancient form of story (associated mainly with Aesop) in which animals behave in a way that is half-human and half-animal. Usually they adopt a human version of their traditional animal qualities.

- <u>Satire</u> is criticism using oblique, frequently amusing means. Though often humorous, satire can be quite vicious and the main intent is to ridicule: many satirists would claim that they wish to reform vices by this ridicule. Orwell ridicules the pursuit of power by placing it in a farmyard.

- An <u>allegory</u> is a story which conceals its main meaning beneath the surface of a quite different narrative. Many people interpret parables in the Bible as allegories. The essential feature of an allegory is that each main person or event in the surface story should have an equivalent in the hidden story.

> **❝*Mr Jones was safely out of the way*❞**

Like the other human characters, **<u>Mr Jones plays a minor role</u>** in the book. Having introduced him as a drunken, neglectful farmer, the narrative concentrates on the animals. Jones's brutality to the animals is the reason why they plan revolution, and later, the threat of his return to Animal Farm helps to reinforce the pigs' authority. His drunkenness is paralleled later by the pigs' over-indulgence in drink. Mrs Jones is introduced with even fewer words; asleep and snoring next to her worthless husband, she seems, by association, to be equally worthless.

Explore

Can you think of reasons why Orwell focused his attention on the animals and gave the humans such minor roles?

Old Major has had a dream important enough to be shared with the other farm animals. From his appearance, and because of his past history, it is obvious that <u>Old Major is greatly admired by the other animals</u>, so they will listen to what he has to say with respect. The name Major itself implies some <u>seniority</u> and <u>rank</u>.

Significantly, Old Major's vision for the future has its origins <u>in a dream</u>. However, it is one thing to have a dream and quite another thing to see it translated into reality. It is ironic that an animal who has apparently been <u>well cared for</u> should be the one who <u>dreams of freedom from human oppression</u>. Like Karl Marx, who spent years in study at the British Museum perfecting his theories, <u>Old Major has had more time to think than most of the animals</u>. It becomes apparent later in the novel that Old Major had not in any way considered that the ideas he presented would be used by others to achieve their own selfish desires.

The mood of <u>the first meeting is optimistic</u>. It establishes the characters of the story and sets the scene for the revolution.

Explore

Consider the extent to which the sheep are a caricature of 'the average people' in society, who do not think for themselves, preferring instead to place blind trust in the decisions of those they believe to be their natural superiors.

<u>The sheep</u> have no individual identity and <u>merely follow whoever directs them</u>; they behave as one would expect a flock of sheep to behave. Note that because of their <u>docile nature</u> they play a crucial part in the story.

21

Boxer the horse has two companions: Clover, a mare, and Benjamin, a donkey. Boxer and Clover are like a long-married couple. <u>Clover</u> is established as a <u>gentle</u> and <u>maternal</u> <u>character</u>. Her most prominent quality is <u>sympathy</u>, in contrast to the callousness of the pigs. Benjamin is <u>cynical</u> <u>about</u> <u>the</u> <u>events</u> <u>both</u> <u>before</u> <u>and</u> <u>after</u> <u>the</u> <u>revolution</u>. He has misgivings about Old Major's dream and about the pigs' later conduct, but <u>does</u> <u>nothing</u> <u>to</u> <u>prevent</u> <u>the</u> <u>abuses</u> <u>that</u> <u>follow</u>. Despite his exterior cynicism, he is <u>deeply</u> <u>devoted</u> <u>to</u> <u>Boxer</u>. The unspoken nature of his affection makes it more convincing, especially when compared with the pigs' frequent, insincere declarations of good intent later in the story.

> **‟Comrades, you have heard about the strange dream”**

Old Major indicates that he is nearing the end of his life. His age and maturity give his words great importance. He graphically describes the life of a farm animal. He uses <u>plain,</u> <u>simple</u> <u>language,</u> with repetition and short sentences that are like <u>slogans</u>: 'no animal in England is free'. Old Major poses a series of questions asking why the animals lead such appalling lives. This a useful <u>rhetorical</u> <u>technique</u> for a speaker to use, as he can provide the right questions and then supply the answers he wants. Thus the animals are not required to think for themselves, merely to agree with what he says.

Explore

Compare Old Major's public-speaking techniques with those used by Squealer later on in the novel.

Old Major moves towards the crux of his speech – <u>the</u> <u>parasitic</u> <u>nature</u> <u>of</u> <u>Man</u>. Man lives off animals but gives them virtually nothing in return. Old Major shows sympathy for the animals' plight and provides examples of Man's exploitation. References to Clover's lost foals and the stolen milk and eggs are calculated to arouse the listening animals' indignation. He then describes in horrific detail the deaths the animals will suffer, particularly Boxer.

This speech is **the equivalent of the Communist Manifesto** by Karl Marx and Friedrich Engels. Man represents the capitalist system, exploiting the labour of the animals/working-classes. The last sentences of the Communist Manifesto are, 'The workers have nothing to lose ... but their chains. They have a world to gain. Workers of the world, unite!' If you read Major's speech carefully, you will find sentences stressing the need for unity, and others that emphasise the animals' state of slavery ('chains').

Old Major aims to **sow the seeds of revolution**, recognising that it will take several generations to achieve his idea of **a utopian society**. He warns the animals to **beware of persuasive but misleading arguments**. Ironically, this first warning is the one they most quickly forget. Things might have turned out differently if they had taken it to heart. Old Major's **use of very simple slogans**, so that even the dullest animal can grasp his message, is **effective but dangerous**. The slogans are **open to various interpretations**, as will later be shown.

The scuffle between the dogs and the rats emphasises the difference between what Old Major says about unity and **the reality of the animals' natural aggression towards each other**. Old Major offers a simple concept: all animals are friends and Man is the common enemy. He forgets that some animals naturally prey upon others. Most importantly of all, he ignores the fact that some animals are cleverer than others. Old Major's **idealism** fails to take account of the practical difficulties involved in creating a new society. He warns the animals that once Man is conquered, **the animals must be careful not to copy Man's vices**.

Text commentary

Explore

Note how ironic this is when set against the later behaviour of the pigs and some of the other animals. Try to decide for yourself which of Old Major's ideals are tossed aside later, and note when each happens.

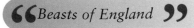
❝❝*Beasts of England* **❞❞**

To conclude his speech, Old Major sings a song, 'Beasts of England'. It has simple, emotional appeal and describes a joyous future for the animals, stressing the positive aspects of their new life. Its simple rhythm and rhyme pattern make it easy to remember and it becomes the animals' revolutionary anthem. <u>'Beasts of England' represents the first great song of Communism, 'The International'</u>, calling on workers of all lands to rise up.

Chapter 2

> **"Three nights later old Major died peacefully in his sleep. "**

The pigs begin to instruct and organise the animals, preparing them for rebellion. The three pigs, Napoleon, Snowball and Squealer are described in some detail.

- **Napoleon**, 'a fierce-looking Berkshire boar', is named after one of Europe's most famous revolutionaries, who turned a popular uprising into a dictatorship.
- **Snowball** is described as 'more vivacious' than Napoleon, but is also considered to have less 'depth of character'. His name implies that he will 'melt away' or be overshadowed by Napoleon. He is the brains behind the principles of Animalism.
- **Squealer** is introduced as a 'brilliant talker'. His name perhaps implies treachery: 'squealer' is slang for someone who will tell secrets under pressure.

Napoleon, Snowball and Squealer translate Old Major's vision into a workable system but encounter **difficulties in communicating it** to the animals. Snowball, for example, tries to explain to Mollie that ribbons and sugar are not as important as oats and hay and must be sacrificed if the revolution is to succeed. It is clear that Mollie is not the stuff from which revolutionaries are made!

<u>Moses</u> <u>the</u> <u>raven</u> was absent during Old Major's assembly in Chapter 1. He is now introduced as Mr Jones's special pet. The author is using Moses as <u>a vehicle</u> <u>to</u> <u>criticise</u> <u>established</u> <u>churches</u> <u>and</u> <u>their</u> <u>teachings</u>, particularly the Christian church. There were very strong ties between the <u>Czars</u> and the <u>Russian</u> <u>Orthodox</u> <u>Church</u>. Each had an interest in <u>preserving</u> <u>tradition</u> and was seen as the <u>enemy</u> <u>of</u> <u>change</u>. Through Moses, the Russian Orthodox Church in particular and Christianity in general are attacked for serving the wishes of the ruling classes. Though the pigs ridicule Moses' ideas here, notice how they later turn them to their advantage.

Explore

What is the significance of Moses' claim that animals go to Sugarcandy Mountain when they die? Is this promise of 'heaven' nothing more than a bribe to ensure obedience?

❝ *Their most faithful disciples* ❞

<u>It</u> <u>is</u> <u>important</u> <u>for</u> <u>the</u> <u>pigs</u> <u>to</u> <u>win</u> <u>the</u> <u>support</u> <u>of</u> <u>Clover</u> <u>and</u> <u>Boxer</u>, as the other animals have great respect for these two animals. Unfortunately, Boxer and Clover lack the intelligence or wit to think for themselves.

❝ *Jones was expelled, and the Manor Farm was theirs* ❞

Mr Jones's harvest was ready for reaping in more ways than one: he reaps the rewards of getting drunk and neglecting his animals. Although the secret meetings helped to put the animals in the right frame of mind for revolution, <u>when</u> <u>the</u> <u>rebellion</u> <u>happens</u> <u>it</u> <u>is</u> <u>a</u> <u>spontaneous</u> <u>response</u> <u>to</u> <u>anger</u> <u>and</u> <u>hunger</u>. Compare the lightness of the first skirmish with the intensity of the later battles. No one is hurt, and the humans look comical rather than tragic as they take to their heels. Mr Jones is expelled quickly and easily by the united animals.

The cruel and humiliating methods which Mr Jones used to keep the animals in submission — nose-rings, dog chains, and so on

— are easy to identify. It is important to realise that Animalism (like Russian Communism) is a response to a real need. This makes the betrayals by Napoleon and Stalin all the more shameful.

Snowball has already expressed his disapproval of ribbons and the vanity which goes with them. At this point he develops his ideas more fully, declaring them the mark of the hated humans and saying that 'All animals should go naked'.

It is significant that Boxer decides to give up his straw hat — not worn for reasons of vanity, but to keep away flies in summer — as a demonstration of his wholehearted support for the revolution. It is typical of Boxer's lack of self-esteem that, under Snowball's influence, he equates his working hat with Mollie's silly ribbons. This is an early indication of Boxer's naivety and readiness for self-sacrifice, and contrasts with the calculated self-interest with which the pigs later go about their work.

It is Snowball who leads the animals to destroy the hated symbols of oppression. Napoleon assumes the significant role of provider by giving food to the animals. Even at this early stage, Napoleon gets a head start in establishing superiority.

The animals are overjoyed as they view the farm, now under their control, from the top of the knoll. Remember this scene later, when the knoll becomes the setting for confessions and executions. Snowball and Napoleon take the lead in entering the farmhouse.

Mollie has to be cautioned about her fondness for ribbons. There is evidently a huge difference in the attitudes and hopes of the different animals. In contrast to the respect shown to the hams, Boxer kicks in the barrel of beer, seen as the cause of much suffering. Keep this in mind when the pigs later indulge their appetite for food and drink in the farmhouse. Here, the pigs decree that no animal shall ever live in the farmhouse.

The entry into the farmhouse is Orwell's version of the famous **attack on the Czar's Winter Palace in Petrograd**. This happened during the October Revolution, but this is one of several alterations to the order of events. The mixture of wonder and disgust at the sights within links the two events.

> **66** *The pigs now revealed that during the past three months they had taught themselves to read and write* **99**

Consider the importance that Snowball gives to **literacy**. In any modern society, a literate, concerned and involved population is **the key to democracy**. When a large section of the community is illiterate, there are difficulties involved in understanding politicians' words, and democratic institutions face real danger from ambitious men.

> **66** *in its place painted ANIMAL FARM* **99**

Napoleon leads the way to Manor Farm gate, but it is Snowball who paints in the name Animal Farm. Notice that, although Napoleon gives the orders, it is Snowball who has the ability to write. Throughout this chapter it becomes increasingly evident that **Napoleon and Snowball have very different ideas** about the demands of power and leadership.

Place names were significant in the Russian Revolution. For instance, the city of St Petersburg had been re-named Petrograd in 1914 to sound less German and more Russian. After the Revolution it was again re-named: Leningrad. Ironically, it has recently returned to the name St Petersburg, just as in the closing pages of *Animal Farm* the name reverts to Manor Farm.

At the next meeting, Snowball and Napoleon introduce **the basic tenets of Animalism** and tell the animals that they are to learn to read and write.

Snowball summarises the ideals of Animalism into Seven Commandments and writes them up on the barn wall for all to read and observe as **'an unalterable law by which all the animals on Animal Farm must live for ever after'**. Although the Seven Commandments are intended as guidelines, they are later exploited and used to manipulate the working animals. Be aware of how and at what point in the story these alterations occur.

Squealer helps to fix the Seven Commandments on the big barn wall. Later in the novel, he will not be content with holding the paint pot, but will actually do the writing himself, **altering the Commandments** to convey whatever meaning the pigs regard as helpful to them at the time.

Already a gap is widening between 'the cleverer ones' and the other animals in their understanding of the Seven Commandments. One of the key insights in *Animal Farm* is that **the language used by governments is sometimes remote from the language of the average man**. Snowball does his best to simplify the system of Animalism into the Seven Commandments and various slogans, but this will not work if the animals are illiterate, are too busy with other matters, are cynical, or are simply uninterested in their own welfare. The later changes made to the Commandments reflect the weakening of Old Major's original ideals and the animals' decline into a way of life worse than anything they experienced under Mr Jones.

In calling for the harvest to be gathered quickly, <u>Snowball</u> <u>shows</u> <u>his</u> <u>practical</u> <u>nature</u>. By contrast, <u>Napoleon</u> <u>takes</u> <u>charge</u> <u>of</u> <u>the</u> <u>milk</u> — the first hint of greed. This is an early indication of how much worse life will be for the animals under his regime. The animals leave the meeting, inspired by their new life.

Chapter 3

> ❝*How they toiled and sweated to get the hay in!*❞

The introductory paragraphs of this chapter indicate how the revolution might have worked. Almost every animal unselfishly and willingly gives of its best. There is <u>total</u> <u>co-operation</u> between them and not a grain is stolen. The animals work just as hard now as they do later under Napoleon's oppressive leadership. These chapters also provide an excellent example of <u>Orwell's</u> <u>skill</u> <u>in</u> <u>applying</u> <u>human</u> <u>activities</u> <u>to</u> <u>animal</u> <u>abilities</u>.

Boxer is essential to the success of the farm, and has such pride in his work that he earns universal respect. Despite these good qualities, he is <u>flawed:</u> <u>his</u> <u>view</u> <u>of</u> <u>life</u> <u>is</u> <u>conditioned</u> <u>by</u> <u>a</u> <u>few</u> <u>simple</u> <u>slogans</u>. By limiting himself in this way, he becomes the unwitting tool of Napoleon's corrupt ambitions to take complete control of the farm.

In contrast, consider how lazy and deceitful <u>Mollie</u> is when work needs to be done. She is an example of someone who would be of little practical use to any social system. <u>The</u> <u>cat</u> is another example of a parasite, feeding on the fruits of others and contributing nothing.

Benjamin remains <u>stubbornly</u> <u>unmoved</u> by the revolution in a way that suggests he has low expectations of the new Animal Farm. Compare his attitude with Boxer's, who expects much.

The green flag with hoof and horn is the exact equivalent of the Soviet flag: the red flag with hammer and sickle (representing industrial and agricultural workers). You will notice in *Animal Farm*, as in real life, many examples of the **symbolic use of flags, decorations and anthems**.

> **But it was noticed that these two were never in agreement**

Napoleon and Snowball, the two leaders, are in open disagreement. Disagreements of this kind do not occur once Snowball has left the farm. The disagreements are not constructive, but occur because different points of view are held by different animals. This is sometimes referred to as **'confrontation politics'**. For all their shortcomings, **open debates** on policy and planning at least take place — they no longer will once Napoleon is in sole command. Any open system of government, however confrontational, self-centred and power-seeking, is better than one where no discussion at all takes place.

Snowball is always busy with schemes that are intended to benefit the animals, but from which they seem to gain little. There seems to be **a gap between Snowball's ideals and the other animals' simple aspirations**. Undeterred by the failure of some of the animals to learn to read and write, Snowball cleverly reduces the principles of Animalism to a slogan that even the dimmest animal can understand: **'Four legs good, two legs bad'**. Unfortunately, the sheep take this simple saying too much to heart and later repeat it mindlessly to frustrate Snowball's good intentions. Squealer seems to have a better understanding of his audience: his later comment, **'surely none of you want Jones back'**, is a more persuasive argument. Note that characters' responses to the new situation are already being characterised by typical behaviour or slogans, such as Boxer's 'I will work harder'. Chart the use of slogans throughout the novel.

It is at this point that the **puppies** are introduced. They are taken away by Napoleon and educated in isolation. Of course, we later learn that **Napoleon** is **indoctrinating them** (teaching them to think the way he wants them to), and the puppies reappear as Napoleon's bodyguards when they chase Snowball from the farm. It is important to note that **Napoleon** **plans** **this** **from** **the** **start**: the birth of the litter coincides with Napoleon's quarrel with Snowball about Snowball's increasing popularity with the other animals.

Explore

Think about examples of indoctrination in today's society. One example might be suicide bombers who are heavily influenced by extremist propaganda.

These **two** **types** **of** **education** are placed side by side for comparison: Napoleon's indoctrination of the puppies and Snowball's literacy classes.

> *The mystery of where the milk went to was soon cleared up.*

The mystery of the disappearing milk is explained. Notice that **Snowball** is **an** **accomplice** **in** **this** **injustice**, and that he yields to the pigs' selfishness in keeping the windfall apples for their own consumption.

When Old Major used it, the word **'comrades'** **implied** **equality** among the animals. Squealer uses the word to conceal the fact that they are no longer equal: 'Comrades! ... You do not imagine, I hope, that we pigs are doing this in a spirit of selfishness or privilege?' The ease with which the animals are duped over something as basic as food shows their **passive** **acceptance** **of** **the** **pigs'** **authority**. From the start, **Squealer** **bullies** **the** **animals** **into** **complying** **with** **the** **pigs'** **orders**. Here, he gives plausible excuses for the pigs' privileged position and authority. In case his 'reasons' fail to convince them, Squealer ends with the question: 'Who wants to see Jones back?' Mr Jones's tyranny is still recent enough for the animals to be persuaded that life under the pigs' authority is preferable.

Uncover the plot

Delete two of the three alternatives given to find the correct plot.

Beware possible misconceptions and muddles.

Mr Pilkington/Mr Jones/Mr Whymper goes to bed drunk and the animals all gather on the knoll/in the farmhouse/in the big barn to hear Old Major/Napoleon/Boxer speak. The pig/horse/dog tells of the misery Man causes animals and preaches patience/tolerance/rebellion; finally he relates his dream of a golden future in a song: 'Animals Arise!'/'Beasts of England'/'Animal Farm'.

Old Major dies, and the animals continue to hold secret meetings organised by the pigs/dogs/horses, the most intelligent animals. The rebellion is highly organised/planned as a military operation/spontaneous; Jones gets drunk again and forgets to feed the animals, so they drive him, his wife and his men off the farm. They bury/burn/throw away all the reins, bits, whips and knives, and enter the farmhouse with triumph/delight/fear.

Napoleon/Snowball/Squealer changes the name of the farm on the gate/front door/barn wall and writes up the Five/Seven/Ten Commandments. The corn/wheat/hay harvest is the best ever and all summer/autumn/winter the animals are happy. On Saturdays/Sundays/Mondays there is no work and their flag is hoisted — a white horn and hoof on a red/blue/green background. Snowball sums up the Commandments as: 'Two/four/six legs good, two/four/six legs bad', which the cows/sheep/hens repeat endlessly.

Snowball and Napoleon/Squealer/Boxer disagree about everything. Napoleon/Squealer/Boxer takes four/seven/nine puppies away to educate them secretly. Apples and milk are reserved for the dogs/horses/pigs.

Chapters 4–7

Chapter 4

> **By the late summer the news of what had happened on Animal Farm had spread**

Mr Jones is portrayed as **weak and slightly ridiculous**, the pub bore who cannot win the sympathy of his neighbours. His character never comes alive in the way that the main animal characters do. The human beings in the story are little more than **caricatures** of unpleasant types of people.

Mr Pilkington of Foxwood and Mr Frederick of Pinchfield are neighbouring farmers who dislike each other as much as they dislike the deposed Mr Jones. Their behaviour is **a reminder of why the revolution happened** at Manor Farm. As neighbouring farmers, they have a vested interest in seeing that the revolution does not succeed. However, being on bad terms with each other, they fail to join forces and overturn it. Later on, **Napoleon makes use of their mutual hostility** to further his own ends.

The revolution at Animal Farm makes the local farmers anxious. They act with considerable brutality to **prevent similar uprisings** on their own farms. Later, however, they trade with and even socialise with the revolutionaries, when they realise that the pigs have become oppressors, just like themselves. The anthem 'Beasts of England' has a rallying effect when sung by animals on the neighbouring farms.

Explore

Even apparently trivial details reflect the precision of Orwell's political commentary. From the beginning, the Russian Revolution produced opposite reactions: from the workers and journalists who saw the future in Communism, to the Western Powers who considered invasion.

> **Battle of the Cowshed**

Mr Jones attempts to recapture the farm, but once more the humans are dispatched relatively easily. The **physical defeat** of

Mr Jones, with his men and their guns, **is** **relatively** **easy** for the animals. They find it **far** **more** **difficult** **to** **overcome** **the** **pigs'** **manipulation** **of** **their** **emotions**.

Snowball's **mastery** **of** **military** **strategy**, his **brilliant** **leadership** and his **personal** **courage** during the Battle of the Cowshed are crucial to the animals' victory. However, his brilliance and success also shows Napoleon how much of a threat Snowball could be to his own ambitions. Ironically, Snowball's military prowess here sows the seeds of his later expulsion from Animal Farm by Napoleon and his henchmen.

The Battle of the Cowshed is another **amusing** **fusion** **of** **the** **animal** **and** **the** **human**. Snowball's tactics may have come from Julius Caesar, but they are put into operation by very animal-like behaviour. See how many examples you can find of animal behaviour being deployed as part of the battle plan.

Benjamin is in the front line of attack at the Battle of the Cowshed. With Benjamin, **actions** **always** **speak** **louder** **than** **words** — unlike the pigs, who promise much but never actually deliver. Despite Benjamin's cynicism, he is the first to join in defending the farm against attack. You should think about why Benjamin does not help to defend the animals against Napoleon's more sinister 'attack' on their revolutionary ideals.

The wounded **Snowball** **demonstrates** **his** **bravery** by attacking Mr Jones. He is the hero of the hour, but notice how easily the animals are led by propaganda to take sides against him later on, even though they witness his extreme bravery here. In contrast to Snowball and Boxer, the names of **Napoleon** **and** **Squealer** **are** **conspicuous** **by** **their** **absence** during the battle and its aftermath. Remember the events of the Battle of the Cowshed as described here, and Snowball's moment of glory, because **Napoleon** **later** **rewrites** **history** to suit his own needs. This is **a** **common** **practice** **of** **dictators**.

The incident with the stable boy indicates Boxer's **physical power**, already demonstrated when he destroyed the beer barrel with one kick earlier in the story. Boxer's **compassion** for the stable boy and his **concern** about what the others think about his action give insights into his character and what is important to him. His words show that he has **no desire to kill anybody**, merely to frighten them. Contrast this with **Snowball's brisk, no-nonsense attitude to casualities** of the battle. Note the maxims he utters from time to time, for example '**The only good human being is a dead one**'. They provide an insight into the way his mind works.

The two major conflicts — the Battles of the Cowshed and the Windmill — come at crucial moments for the animals. Led by Snowball, the Battle of the Cowshed is **co-ordinated and united.** They are **proud and dignified in victory**. They need no reassurance, and make their own decisions as to who should get the honours. After the **Battle of the Windmill**, they are **depressed and weary**, needing reassurance from Squealer. The victory celebrations after the later battle are **carefully contrived** with songs, speeches and the firing of a gun, followed by the drunken debauchery of the pigs.

Chapter 5

> ❝*In January there came bitterly hard weather.*❞

The **mood of the novel darkens** in this chapter. At the beginning, Orwell deals with a small-scale personal problem: Clover counselling Mollie and Mollie's desertion. This is no real loss and fits into a pattern of some animals failing to adjust to the new society. The account of Snowball planning the windmill is respectfully humorous. However, by the end of this chapter, Napoleon calls to the dogs and the terror begins.

Signs of social change and division are becoming apparent at Animal Farm. The pigs now decide all questions of farm policy. At first their decisions have to be agreed by a majority vote, but later this sole remaining check on the pigs' power is discarded. A gulf has opened between Snowball and Napoleon that becomes public during the meetings. You should note their very different leadership styles.

Snowball wins popularity with 'his brilliant speeches', but fails to see the danger posed by Napoleon. We are also told that, although he wins the hearts of the animals, he often fails to gain their votes. Snowball's plan to build a windmill to take the drudgery out of the animals' lives exemplifies his technical ingenuity, enterprise and concern for the animals' welfare.

Napoleon spends his time criticising Snowball's plans and making sure that the majority vote goes his way. The sheep play a crucial role in this. Napoleon manipulates them to disrupt Snowball's speeches and later on to shout down all who oppose him. Their inability to think for themselves and the way they allow themselves to be manipulated at the meetings mean that the sheep play a vital part in Napoleon's rise to power. Napoleon's crude rejection of the windmill plans by urinating over them tells us a great deal about him. It is a coarse comment both on the nature of Napoleon's leadership and on the way that intellectuals are often treated by oppressive dictatorships.

"The animals formed themselves into two factions"

The windmill becomes such an important and controversial issue that it divides the animals. Compare the slogans of Snowball's and Napoleon's supporters. Snowball's vision of the animals' society of the future involves less work. Given the pigs' greed, it is perhaps predictable that Napoleon's slogan should concentrate on food. Notice its irony: whoever eats well later on, it is certainly not the working animals.

Explore

Think about the function of propaganda. When else in history, apart from the Russian Revolution, has propaganda been used effectively to make people feel as though they should act in a certain way?

The debate about defence finds parallels in our own society. Unfortunately, because of the way in which political debate at Animal Farm has degenerated into a matter of simple opposition of whatever the other party is saying, the animals are unable to make a balanced choice between the different points of view. Snowball is keen to use propaganda to spread the revolutionary ideas, but fails to see that Napoleon uses exactly the same techniques to undermine Snowball's position with the animals. Afterwards, when he has driven Snowball from the farm, Napoleon uses these propaganda techniques to blacken Snowball's name and to distort the animals' memory of him.

It is clear from the beginning that Napoleon has made up his mind that his power will never be secure while it can be threatened by so eloquent and persuasive a speaker as Snowball. The brevity of Napoleon's windmill speech is a foretaste of the speed and brutality of his final response. Snowball tries to use argument and reason to persuade the animals to support the building of the windmill. He understands its potential for transforming the animals' lives. Compare Snowball's sincerity and concern for the common good with Napoleon's hypocrisy and self-interest later in the story. Here, Napoleon's quiet confidence suggests that he has planned the imminent attack.

Snowball's passionate appeal for the windmill triggers Napoleon's signal for the dogs' attack, emphasising the importance of the windmill as an issue. This key scene is something of a watershed. The mood of the animals' meetings changes from now on. The atmosphere becomes one of threat and fear, rather than of hope.

Snowball's banishment leaves the animals at Napoleon's mercy and his <u>reign of terror and bloodshed begins</u>. Not one of the animals had the presence of mind to ask Napoleon what he was doing with the puppies which he had taken into his care. Napoleon's <u>gradual change into a 'human'</u> is foreshadowed in the way the dogs obey him, just as <u>other dogs used to obey Mr Jones</u>. The pigs now separate themselves from the other animals and take over the management of farm affairs.

The atmosphere of the meetings is also different from now on. The reference to the platform from which Old Major first spoke to the animals is a reminder of the way his <u>ideals have been betrayed by Napoleon</u>. At the Sunday meeting, what used to be an occasion for the animals to allocate work for the week has been changed into a time when they receive their orders. The <u>freedom to debate</u>, and therefore to disagree, is <u>done away with</u> in a moment, and with it goes freedom of choice: the very thing the animals rebelled for. Saluting the flag and singing the anthem is no longer a pleasure, but a duty.

Explore

One way you could chart the collapse of Animalism is to draw a timeline to show when each of the ideals is destroyed.

Some of the animals are unhappy at the turn of events, but they are <u>unable to express their thoughts clearly</u>. Four young porkers begin a protest but back down in the face of threats from the dogs. Napoleon later ensures that they pay the ultimate price for their opposition to him. The dogs' threatening growls and the sheeps' mindless bleating prevent anyone from voicing further concern.

None of the animals question whether Comrade Napoleon believes that all animals are equal. Nor do they object to the idea that, while they might make mistakes, Napoleon cannot. Suddenly, <u>Napoleon has become more than just an animal</u>.

"Squealer spoke so persuasively**"**

Squealer becomes prominent in the organisation of the new society.

As his **spokesman**, Squealer ensures that Napoleon becomes even more unapproachable and secure. **The crucial importance of literacy and intelligence in the fight against oppression is shown here**. Consider the skill with which Squealer subtly puts over lies, half-truths and omissions to keep the animals in docile agreement with the pigs' plans for them. If they had been less obedient and more confident of their own abilities, the other animals might have stood a chance against Squealer. Squealer's frequent question: 'Who wants Jones back?' reinforces whatever argument he is trying to put across. This is the ultimate threat and is increasingly the only point upon which the pigs and the other animals are in agreement.

Boxer and the other animals begin to **doubt their own memories** and believe Squealer's lies instead. His brain unused to thinking, Boxer decides that Napoleon's words must be true. Given the position of respect in which the other animals hold him, Boxer's maxim, **'Napoleon is always right'**, is disastrous. His other maxim, **'I will work harder'**, shows that he assumes hard work will solve every problem. Hard work counts for little if it is unthinkingly applied: in many ways, **Boxer oppresses himself** by his refusal to use his intellect.

Explore

Note how Boxer's loyalty is rewarded later in the novel. He is sent to the knacker's yard.

The announcement that the windmill is to be built after all comes as a surprise to the animals after Napoleon's opposition to it. This is a calculated move: by announcing that the windmill is to be built, Napoleon turns the animals' attention away from the other announcements which say that during the next two years the animals must work hard for smaller rations of food.

Text commentary

"The animals ... accepted his explanation"

Explore

Note how the end of this chapter signifies a major turning point in the novel. For the first time evil is practised openly.

This chapter identifies very clearly the groups that maintain Napoleon's position as dictator. The <u>sheep</u> <u>are</u> <u>the</u> <u>mindless</u> <u>supporters</u>, but the final lines show two other elements at work. The history of Snowball is already being re-written and the animals believe all, thanks to <u>Squealer's</u> <u>persuasion</u> (the propaganda machine, together with the newly-mentioned Minimus) and <u>the</u> <u>threats</u> <u>of</u> <u>the</u> <u>dogs</u> (secret police).

Chapter 6

"All that year the animals worked like slaves."

Explore

Look at the way a totalitarian dictatorship has been assembled, with its fawning courtiers, arbitrary law enforcement, distortions of truth and maintenance of rule through fear.

The novel can be seen as falling into two halves. Chapters 1 to 5 deal with the rebellion and a new, democratic way of life for the animals on the farm. At the beginning of Chapter 6, the animals are again living under tyrannical rule — although they reassure themselves that all is well because at least they are not working for a 'pack of idle, thieving human beings'. But who are they really working for? Chapters 6 to 10 show how their lives become harder and harder, while the pigs transform themselves precisely into a 'pack of idle, thieving human beings'.

The building of the windmill involves <u>enormous</u> <u>effort</u> from the animals, especially Boxer. Boxer's Herculean efforts to move the boulders uphill begin to tell on his physique. His strength and belief in the ideals of the revolution help him to carry out the work, but <u>his</u> <u>reliance</u> <u>on</u> <u>maxims</u> <u>limits</u> <u>his</u> <u>understanding</u> of what is happening to himself and to the other animals on the farm.

The 'new policy' of <u>trading with neighbouring farms effectively breaks the animals' First Commandment</u>. As before, an announcement about the windmill is used to distract attention from the announcement about Napoleon's trading activities involving the sale of the hens' eggs. Allowing no discussion, <u>Squealer simply informs individual animals of decisions already taken</u>. Any opposition is silenced by using the sheep's disruption at meetings and by threatening any individual who voices opposition.

Note the pride the animals take in the fact that '<u>on all fours</u>' Napoleon gives orders to <u>Mr Whymper</u>. Mr Whymper's involvement with the farm is crucial to the development of Napoleon's relationships with the neighbouring farmers. The employment of Whymper is one of several instances demonstrating the fact that <u>Animal Farm is becoming accepted by the neighbouring farmers</u>, though not approved.

The rest of the animals might not have attained Utopia, but with the pigs now <u>moving into the farmhouse and sleeping in beds</u>, it would appear that they have achieved an ambition of sorts. Squealer's use of 'Leader' for Napoleon also adds to the distance between the pigs and the other animals and is part of <u>the developing ceremonial around Napoleon</u>.

<u>Squealer's arguments are repetitive</u>: he feels no need to vary his style of presentation. His justification for using one of Mr Jones's beds by defining it merely as a place to sleep, ignores the luxuriousness and unnaturalness of a human bed as a place for an animal to sleep. Equally false is the distinction he draws between sheets and blankets. <u>The animals find such arguments difficult to refute</u>. Someone with Snowball's intelligence might have seen the <u>gaping holes in Squealer's arguments</u>.

Clover vaguely remembers some of the original revolutionary ideals and she tries to check the Commandments, but she has to ask **Muriel** to read them to her. The **changes in the Commandments** puzzle her but, because it is written down, she accepts it. This is the first specific amendment to the Seven Commandments, **a major part of the re-writing of history**. This time it occurs mysteriously; think how it later becomes obvious what is happening.

The **windmill** gives the animals a sense of **purpose and commitment.** Apart from its mechanical benefits, it might also give them a **sense of equality** with human society. It is important, too, **in developing Napoleon's status among the other farmers**. The ruin of the windmill is disastrous for the animals, though in one sense helpful to Napoleon. It assists his policy of treating **Snowball as an enemy of the state** who can absorb blame for any failures of the leadership. Like most dictators, Napoleon is unable to admit to any mistakes or errors of judgement. In Snowball, he now has someone whom he can blame for whatever goes wrong or for whatever mistakes he makes. Snowball is also used as an awful **example to the rest of the animals** of what happens to those who oppose Napoleon. The witch-hunt for Snowball distracts them from more serious matters.

Chapter 7

❝The animals carried on as best they could❞

Both sides of the new animal society find inspiration in Boxer's strength: the pigs for purposes of exploitation and propaganda, the other animals for reassurance. Suddenly, the simple 'virtues' framed in the Seven Commandments take second place to **the need to survive**. Napoleon's deceitfulness misleads Mr Whymper so that public confidence in Animal Farm is maintained. Ironically, the animals' self-sacrifice in supporting

Napoleon's deception of Mr Whymper helps to keep him in power and continues the erosion of the revolution's original ideals.

Napoleon is becoming increasingly remote. The ceremonial nature of his infrequent appearances at the Sunday meetings distances him from the days when he was just one of the animals. Squealer, the 'propaganda machine', is increasingly the only contact the animals have with the elite class of pigs.

The **hens' revolt** is doomed to failure from the start. Note how it passes unremarked by Boxer, Clover, Benjamin or any other of the animals. **Each animal is now too self-absorbed to worry about the hens.** Boxer's obsession with using his strength for only one purpose is a good example of this. The animals no longer look 'outward' to the needs of all their fellow animals, only 'inward' to what they consider important for themselves. Napoleon's success in requisitioning the hens' eggs is another defeat for the revolution's high ideals. The idea of trading presupposes that there is a surplus to be traded with, which contradicts Old Major's teaching. Perhaps Orwell is pointing out the **genuine difficulties of putting ideals into practice**.

Explore

The hens' revolt is a clear demonstration of the lengths to which Napoleon is willing to go to quell any type of rebellion. What effect does this have on the other animals?

Napoleon steps up the **witch-hunt** for Snowball, using him to excuse his own indecision about the sale of the timber. The animals are persuaded that Snowball is responsible for the petty annoyances that occur on the farm. Any animal suspected of allegiance to Snowball, and therefore betrayal of Napoleon, is under threat. This practice is, again, a feature of dictatorships.

❝ I do not believe that. ❞

At last, Boxer questions Squealer's reinterpretation of the past. Bluntly, **Boxer challenges Squealer** and refuses to back down. However, when Squealer quotes Comrade Napoleon's

confirmation of the story, **Boxer immediately accepts the new version of events**. Napoleon's position is now so far above ordinary animals that his word is taken, unquestioningly, as gospel. Boxer's disagreement has, however, been noted by Squealer who now sees him as a **potential threat** to the security of the pigs' power.

The manipulation of <u>historical evidence</u>, both written and remembered, is essential to Squealer's success. The only things the animals possess are their memories and the original Seven Commandments. Squealer offers written evidence to support his condemnation of Snowball, knowing that, because of the animals' illiteracy, such 'evidence' is worthless to them. His taunt, '<u>if you were able to read</u>', shows his callousness.

<u>Napoleon uses medals to enhance his public image</u>. None represents any real act of bravery, but their cosmetic effect is to raise him above the rest of the animals. Napoleon's guard dogs attack Boxer shortly after he defends Snowball's memory, yet he seems unable to grasp that Napoleon planned this attack on him.

After the bloody and <u>public execution</u> of the pigs, the animals' hysteria makes them confess to 'crimes' which are mere fantasies. <u>Show-trials</u> in modern, real-life dictatorships provide evidence of similar public confessions, especially by those who have nothing to gain from them.

The animals return to the knoll, looking for comfort and reassurance. Boxer, though shocked by the confessions and executions, misses the significance of what has happened and again falls back on his resolution to work harder.

Squealer makes light work of <u>banning 'Beasts of England'</u>. In abolishing the anthem, Napoleon demonstrates his awareness of its potential danger. The new <u>song emphasises loyalty</u> and the animals' duty to Animal Farm.

Uncover the plot

Delete two of the three alternatives given to find the correct plot.

Beware possible misconceptions and muddles.

The fame of Animal Farm grows and, in particular, its flag/song/ Commandments. In August/September/October, the hens/pigeons/ geese bring news that Jones is leading an attack. He is defeated with only one/a few/two animal(s) killed. Snowball and Napoleon/Benjamin/ Boxer are given medals for bravery.

Mollie/Muriel/Clover is the first animal to desert the farm. The frequent disagreements between Snowball and Napoleon/Benjamin/Boxer reach a climax over the construction of the farm/sowing/windmill. The animals are swept away by Snowball's/Napoleon's/Squealer's eloquent pleading, but are prevented from voting for him by Napoleon's dogs who chase him away/kill him/injure him. Napoleon assumes power and abolishes Sunday meetings/the singing of 'Beasts of England'/debates.

Two/three/four weeks later, he announces that the windmill will be built after all, over two/three/four years. Clover/Muriel/Boxer works the hardest in this task. Mr Frederick/Mr Whymper/Mr Pilkington is appointed to act as an intermediary in trading with humans. In September/October/November, a storm/an attack by Jones/Snowball destroys the windmill and building begins again. Food is scarce and eggs are/wheat is/wood is sold to acquire it; meanwhile, Old Major/Jones/Snowball is blamed for everything that goes wrong.

Chapters 8–10

Chapter 8

> **"No** *animal shall kill any other animal without cause* **"**

Muriel again helps Clover by reading the Sixth Commandment to her. As always, Clover can remember more clearly than the others, but not quite clearly enough. The general inability to read and write has ensured that there has only ever been <u>one copy of the Commandments</u>, so there is <u>nothing to verify what they originally said</u>. Remember the tremendous importance which Snowball attached to literacy.

Napoleon now distances himself from the other animals, even the pigs. He has used Animalism and the revolution to <u>feed his ego</u> and has instituted a regime which will serve his every wish. His <u>authority is now absolute</u>. The hens' 'conspiracy' is simply an excuse for the pigs to carry out a <u>ritual slaughter</u>. Its purpose is to provide <u>a public demonstration of their power</u> and so to keep the other animals in fear and terror. It is intended to deter animals who might be contemplating revolution. The death of a few hens out of so many will not have any adverse affect on egg production and is not so controversial as the deaths of Boxer or Clover might have been. It is typical of such a society that <u>the weakest are the most oppressed</u>.

Napoleon's public declaration that he is to sell timber to Pilkington is accompanied by a series of <u>rumours</u> about Frederick's cruelty to his animals. These rumours are similar to those about Animal Farm which were spread in its early days. The details sound like a product of Squealer's propaganda machine. The rumours are put about to provide 'justification' for

Text commentary

Napoleon's decision to deal with Pilkington rather than with Frederick. As yet, the reader has not met Frederick and Pilkington face to face. Most of what we know of them is hearsay.

Note Squealer's sinister role in the post-revolution society — emphasised here by **the 'suicide' of the gander**. The 'suicides' of political activists form another feature of oppressive regimes. Apart from work, the only social events at the farm are the continued blackening of Snowball's character, death-threat slogans directed against Frederick and news of plots and suicide. Compare this with the hive of creative activity which Snowball encouraged. The animals' **social and cultural environment is dreary** indeed.

The **completion of the windmill** is a triumph for the animals, but it presents something of a problem for Napoleon. Until now he has been able to keep the animals occupied with this tremendous enterprise so as not to give them time to consider their situation. **Napoleon identifies himself with the success of the windmill** by appearing at the ceremony in order to name it 'Napoleon Mill'.

Frederick removes the timber from Animal Farm with almost indecent haste. In **Frederick**, Napoleon seems to have met his **equal in ruthlessness**. In an endeavour to salvage prestige among the animals, Napoleon pronounces the death sentence on Frederick. Perhaps Napoleon has made the mistake of thinking that he is dealing with illiterate, bemused animals rather than with **a fellow 'dictator'**.

Explore

This section is a good example of Orwell's ability to write both a story about animals and a political satire.

The bargaining with Pilkington and Frederick, coupled with a propaganda war against whoever is out of favour, echoes Stalin's dealings with Hitler's Germany and the West in the late 1930s. **Napoleon's deal with Frederick** matches **Stalin's pact with Hitler,** which was also followed by betrayal and invasion. Due to characters like Boxer we feel sympathy for the animals. Yet, even though we hate the regime, we are still led to appreciate Orwell's precise reflection of real-life events.

During **the Battle of the Windmill**, Napoleon seems unable to cope for the first time. The superior weapons used by the humans easily repel the animals. This time Boxer and Napoleon come together in the defence of the farm, as Boxer and Snowball did in the Battle of the Cowshed. The destruction of the windmill by Frederick justifies Napoleon's warnings to the animals about the threat posed by humans. It helps us to understand why they continue to tolerate Napoleon's domination.

The Battle of the Windmill **unites the animals in one last effort**. The mood of this battle is quite different, with its 'savage, bitter' fighting resulting in a high casualty rate. Despite his courage when the windmill is blown up, Napoleon is soon back in his accustomed place, directing operations from the rear while the battle is being fought.

Squealer's actions again contradict his words. Although absent from the battle, he claims it a glorious victory for the long-suffering animals. However, Boxer's memory of the battle is still fresh, and he challenges Squealer. For the first time, **Boxer appears to be thinking about the implications of what has happened**.

The **post-battle propaganda** by Napoleon, and the whisky celebration by the pigs, which excludes the working animals, show **the division between the leaders and the led**. Alcohol caused the animals to suffer in the past. Has this really been a 'victory' of the pigs over the animals?

Does the drunken Napoleon reveal his true ambition by **wearing <u>Farmer Jones's bowler hat</u>**? Typical of his now bankrupt leadership is Napoleon's 'illness', obviously a severe hangover, and the resultant decree that <u>**drinking alcohol**</u> is punishable by death. This decree is soon annulled when it is announced that Napoleon has ordered brewing equipment. Animal Farm is now being run for the convenience of the pigs. Even Napoleon's hangover is blamed on Snowball. The pigs' contempt for the animals' welfare is further shown when Napoleon uses the intended retirement grazing ground to grow barley from which whisky can be made.

> **" *a strange incident which hardly anyone was able to understand* "**

Look at the detailed description of what the animals see when they investigate the cause of the loud crash. With the evidence of Squealer's activities so plain, the animals' casual reaction is almost unbelievable. It shows the degree to which **<u>they are now unable to think for themselves</u>**. Only Benjamin still has the presence of mind to realise what is going on. Muriel's unquestioning acceptance of the new Fifth Commandment highlights the fact that **<u>the animals no longer trust their own memories.</u>**

Chapter 9

> **" *Boxer refused to take even a day off work* "**

Despite their callous treatment by the pigs, the animals still have real concern for each other. Boxer's unselfishness and pride in his work again cause concern to his lifelong companions, Clover and Benjamin. Again, **<u>Boxer dreams of the completion of the windmill</u>** and the fulfilment of **<u>a promised retirement</u>**.

The use of **Jones's** **return** **as** **a** **threat** is still effective in subduing the animals, as is **the** **comparison** **between** **post-revolution** **life** **and** **the** **bad** **old** **days** under Farmer Jones. By now, the animals are too confused to trust their own memories, after submitting to so much propaganda and so many distortions of the truth.

The young pigs are kept apart from the other animals and are trained to become the new elite. Note how the privileges and status which the pigs now enjoy create **a** **'superior'** **class** within the animals' society. It is clear that **Napoleon's** **standard** **of** **living** **far** **exceeds** **that** **enjoyed** **by** **Farmer** **Jones**. In some respects, Old Major was right when he said the animals could manage the farm better than Man. But he failed to allow for the worst side of the pigs' character coming into play so strongly, or for the different levels of ambition and ability among the various animals.

Notice how wistfully the animals long for better treatment from the pigs. Notice too how brutally indifferent the pigs are to the emotions of the working animals. Compare this with Jones's careless kindness in putting surplus milk in the hens' mash.

Though this chapter contains one of the most moving incidents of the novel, the death of Boxer, much of it consists of descriptions of what life is like now that a certain stability has come to Animal Farm and the dictatorship remains unchallenged. Squealer's **propaganda** reaches new heights, with his **'readjustment'** **of** **rations** and **documentary** **proof** that the animals are not short of food. Hand in hand with propaganda goes **ceremonial**. Again you can find several examples, but the most striking is probably **the** **compulsory** **Spontaneous** **Demonstration** which echoes the dramatic military parades in Red Square, Moscow.

Moses returns to Animal Farm and tells the animals of the delights of Sugarcandy Mountain. Remember that Moses represents, to some extent, Orwell's view of the more corrupt aspects of organised religion. The pigs, like Jones, treat Moses like a pet. The pigs are quite happy for the animals to **spend their time striving for a better afterlife**, so long as it doesn't affect their work here and now. In addition, they perhaps welcome the **distraction** that Moses provides, as it helps the animals to forget their empty bellies.

Boxer's **physical decline** comes at a time when the pigs' power is virtually unchallenged and the revolutionary ideals, at least for the majority of the animals, are long-forgotten. All that Boxer can look forward to is his retirement. Squealer's response to Boxer's illness gives the animals a moment of concern. However, Squealer has little difficulty in reassuring them.

Benjamin **demonstrates his love for Boxer** by staying with him and keeping the flies away. No doubt he feels he is being very helpful, but certainly it **would have been more helpful if he'd tried to warn the animals**, particularly Boxer, about the pigs' erosion of their revolutionary ideals.

Napoleon shows his **callousness** and his **indifference to suffering** in his **premeditated disposal of Boxer**. Even for the sake of a public relations exercise he cannot bring himself to visit Boxer, merely ordering a bottle of pink medicine from Jones's medicine chest to be sent over — medicine that is of little use to Boxer.

> **❝They are taking Boxer to the knacker's!❞**

Benjamin pushes Muriel aside and reads the clearly written message out to the assembled animals. **For so long inactive, when he does stir himself to action it is too late**. Clover races after the van and calls Boxer to try and escape — but in vain.

The death of Boxer is full of ironies: the fact that Benjamin finally acts decisively and displays passion and anguish, only to be ignored until it is too late, is just one of them. There is the fact that <u>Boxer is taken to his death by his own kind</u> who are too 'stupid' and 'ignorant' to respond, but who could be seen as doing their duty. Of course, there is the irony that <u>Boxer's strength has been spent in the service of Animal Farm</u> and now he lacks the power to break out of the van. The knacker's van which takes Boxer is horribly <u>reminiscent of the mobile extermination vans used by Hitler to transport Jews to the concentration camps</u>.

Explore

Watch this scene in the animated film version of the novel. The animals (aside from Benjamin) are simply unaware of what is happening to Boxer. It is probably the most moving moment in both the novel and the film.

In the speech he makes after Boxer has been taken away, Squealer is at his most hypocritical, callous and cunning. Quickly <u>glossing over Boxer's death</u>, he merely uses it as an excuse for a hymn in praise of Napoleon. Napoleon takes care to <u>associate himself with the grief</u> felt by the animals at Boxer's death and he expediently <u>reminds them of Boxer's two maxims</u>. The pigs have organised Boxer's death and they are the only animals who derive benefit from it, although they manage hypocritical tributes to his memory.

Chapter 10

> **❝A time came when there was no one who remembered ❞**

The windmill is at last complete. Look back to Snowball's original vision of the benefits it would bring the animals and compare it with the reality.

<u>The animals cling to Old Major's vision and 'Beasts of England' is sung in secret</u>. Perhaps the revolution is coming full circle? Squealer takes the sheep away to learn a new song, a preparation for the pigs' abandonment of animal

Text commentary

status: a reminder, perhaps, of Napoleon removing the puppies to 'educate' them.

The appearance of Napoleon, <u>walking on two legs and carrying a whip in his trotter</u>, openly shows the true nature of his power. He has finally achieved what he most envied in man — to be able to walk on two legs. Once again, the animals' protest is drowned by the sheep's carefully rehearsed chanting.

> **❝SOME ANIMALS ARE MORE EQUAL THAN OTHERS❞**

Ironically, the first time <u>Benjamin is persuaded to read aloud,</u> he reads the death-knell of the animals' revolutionary ideals. He, of all the animals, is the most likely to understand the implications of what the remaining Commandment says, yet he makes no comment. Why?

Napoleon now wears Farmer Jones's clothes: he has succeeded in replacing him in every respect. This foreshadows the final scene of the novel, when Napoleon is indistinguishable from his insolent human guests. Having received Pilkington's praise for the wretched conditions endured by the animals, <u>Napoleon removes the last of the revolution's effects</u>: the animals are no longer to address each other as 'Comrade'; the parades to honour Old Major are to be abandoned (his skull has already been buried); the flag is to be changed to a plain green. The signs are that <u>the future for the animals will be far worse than anything they knew under Farmer Jones.</u> Things come <u>full circle</u> with the renaming of the farm, Manor Farm.

> **❝already it was impossible to say which was which.❞**

The final vision, presented through Clover's dim old eyes, is of pigs and men becoming <u>indistinguishable</u>. Does Clover

Explore

Make sure you can express your own opinions about the lessons today's society should learn from *Animal Farm*.

understand the betrayal that has taken place? <u>**The cycle of corruption is complete.**</u> For the animals, it seems there is little to choose between one master and another. The story ends as it began, with the masters of Animal Farm drinking too much, but this time the animals hear no optimistic dream of a new future with a just society. '<u>**All power corrupts, and absolute power corrupts absolutely**</u>.' (Lord Acton)

Uncover the plot

Delete two of the three alternatives given to find the correct plot.

Beware possible misconceptions and muddles.

Napoleon continues to become less tyrannical/accessible/reasonable. He plays Pilkington/Whymper/Jones and Frederick against each other over the proposed sale of eggs/land/timber, and is disappointed/hysterical/enraged when he discovers he has been tricked.

Frederick/Pilkington/Jones attacks the farm and destroys the windmill with gunpowder/sledgehammers/bulldozers. Six animals are killed but the humans are defeated. To celebrate, the pigs drink rum/gin/whisky. Boxer/Benjamin/Napoleon has injured his leg/hoof/back but is due to retire on his 10th/11th/12th birthday. Rations are reduced/adjusted/increased and Animal Farm becomes a monarchy/Republic/Democracy.

Benjamin/Clover/Boxer collapses and is sold to the slaughterhouse by the pigs/humans/other horses, who hold a memorial service/banquet/meeting in his honour.

Weeks/months/years pass and the farm grows richer/poorer/smaller. Many/few/none of the animals remember life before the rebellion and they still have pride/joy/comfort in their farm. This is destroyed when the pigs begin to wear clothes/stand upright/walk on their hind legs. Only one/two/three of the Commandments remain(s) and in the final scene, pigs and humans are shown in a serious meeting/at a party/at a dance. Animal Farm is now to be called Napoleon Farm/Windmill Farm/Manor Farm. When the pigs and men start to agree/argue/drink together, they become indistinguishable from each other.

- The first essential requirement is thorough revision. If you are studying for an 'open book' examination, you will have time to look up quotations and references, but only if you know where to look.

- Read the questions carefully, making sure you underline key words that tell you what to do, e.g 'compare', 'contrast', 'explore', 'explain'. Retelling the story will get you no credit.

- Jot down the main points, **make an essay plan** that shows what you are going to include in each paragraph, then stick to it (see page 62). Make sure you link the paragraphs to each other and refer back to the question so as not to digress.

- Summarise in your introduction how you plan to approach the question, then jump straight into your argument. Ensure you answer *all* of the question, not just part of it.

- Take care with spelling, punctuation and grammar. Avoid using slang or abbreviations. Write in paragraphs, starting a new line and indenting quotations of more than a few words.

- Quotations should be used to increase the clarity of your answer, but extended quotations (more than a few sentences) are usually unhelpful.

- It is important to back up what you say. Remember: **point–quotation–comment** (see page 58). This will ensure that your work stays analytical.

- Finally, use your conclusion to sum up your points and relate them back to the question. If you have missed something, put it in now. Leave five minutes to proofread your work for mistakes.

- Timing is not so crucial for coursework essays, so this is your chance to show what you can really do without having to write under pressure.

- You can obviously go into far more detail than you are able to in an examination. Essays will generally be expected to be 1000–1500 words in length, but follow the advice of your teacher.

- You should develop an argument, avoiding becoming too narrative. **Make an essay plan** and stick to it (see page 62). Refer back to the question while writing the essay to avoid digressing. When writing a comparative piece, the comparison should be made throughout the essay, not just at the end.

- Use your plan to decide what each paragraph is about, as far as possible signalling this to the reader in the opening sentence (often called a topic sentence), this will ensure that your work remains focused on the question.

- It is essential to make reference to the novel being an allegory of the Russian Revolution. Parallels to the political situation are of vital importance.

- As with examination essays, use quotations frequently but carefully, and try to introduce them smoothly. It is often effective to quote just one or two words.

- Make sure your conclusion summarises your arguments. Only at this stage can you consider giving your opinion (e.g. 'I think'). The main body of the essay should not contain personal pronouns.

- Take advantage of being able to draft your essay so that the neat copy is as polished as possible. Don't forget to proofread.

- It is a good idea, if possible, to word process your essay. This will enable you to make changes and improvements to your final draft more easily.

Writing essays

Key quotations

The following are examples of **points, quotations** and **comments** that could be used in an essay on *Animal Farm*.

 Old Major has a dream about a world where the animals are responsible for their own lives and no longer work for man. It is an ideal for a better life:

> *I merely repeat, remember always your duty of enmity towards Man and all his ways. Whatever goes upon two legs, is an enemy. Whatever goes upon four legs, or has wings, is a friend.*

He warns the animals not to fight among themselves but to unite in their hatred of man and free themselves from his oppressive regime.

2 Immediately, it becomes apparent that Napoleon will be a force to be reckoned with once the animals have overthrown the humans:

> *Napoleon was a large, fierce-looking Berkshire boar, the only Berkshire on the farm, not much of a talker, but with a reputation for getting his own way.*

He immediately seems to be different to the other animals and sounds like an imposing figure. Even under the rule of humans he has been getting his own way. The reader can tell that this is likely to continue to be the case.

3 Snowball explains the Seven Commandments in one sentence for those animals who cannot read or understand easily:

> **"FOUR LEGS GOOD, TWO LEGS BAD."**

This is a very simplistic version of what is written but is accessible to all the animals. It is the fact that the pigs are the most educated that allows them to gain supremacy over the other animals.

4 Napoleon rules through fear and crushes any chance of rebellion by murdering a few rebels as an example to others:

> **"He ordered the hens' rations to be stopped, and decreed that any animal giving so much as one grain of corn to a hen should be punished by death. The dogs saw to it that these orders were carried out."**

Napoleon incites fear in the animals and enforces his threats through his own version of the secret police, the dogs he has trained to serve him. He establishes a regime that cannot easily be threatened.

5 By the end of the novel there is no difference between the pigs and the men:

> **"The creatures outside looked from pig to man, and from man to pig, and from pig to man again; but already it was impossible to say which was which."**

The novel has gone in a full circle and the animals' ideas of equality are shattered. They are even more helpless than at the start of the novel.

1 In Chapter 2 there were Seven Commandments. By Chapter 10 there is only one Commandment: 'ALL ANIMALS ARE EQUAL, BUT SOME ARE MORE EQUAL THAN OTHERS.' Describe and explain how the Seven Commandments were replaced by one.

2 Animal Farm is subtitled 'A Fairy Story'. It was published in 1945 at the end of the Second World War. What do you think the novel says about the time it was written and other times in history?

3 Compare and contrast the ways in which **two** of the following characters deal with their situation on the farm:

- Napoleon
- Snowball
- Boxer
- Mollie
- Squealer

You should consider:

- their motives
- their methods of trying to achieve what they want
- what Orwell wants you to think about them.

4 How does the character of Squealer exercise control over the other animals?

5 'All power tends to corrupt. Absolute power corrupts absolutely'. To what extent can this be said of Animal Farm?

6 How could the character of Benjamin have altered the situation faced by the animals at the end of the novel?

7 To what extent does Animal Farm end where it began?

8 Discuss why the revolution is ultimately unsuccessful.

9 What is Orwell trying to show the reader through the characters of Boxer and Clover? Can they be blamed for their own situation?

10 Why do you think the animals' revolution ends in failure?

11 To what extent is the novel nothing more than an allegory for the Russian Revolution?

12 Discuss the ways in which Napoleon gains power and then creates and maintains his dictatorship.

13 Compare the approaches of Snowball and Napoleon to leadership and power. Would Snowball have made a better leader?

14 Explore the descent of Animalism from the ideals from which it began to its unrecognisable state by the end of the novel. Could it ever have worked?

15 Orwell claimed his purpose in writing Animal Farm was 'to fuse political and artistic purpose into one whole'. To what extent do you think he succeeded?

16 Discuss to what degree propaganda is responsible for the success of Napoleon's dictatorship.

17 Why do you think that Orwell used animals as his characters when writing Animal Farm?

18 How important is it that the characters are fully developed throughout the novel? Could it be argued that they are two dimensional but that this does not matter?

19 What lesson should the reader learn from reading Animal Farm?

20 In your opinion, is it possible for all animals to be equal or will some always be more equal than others?

Spidergram essay plans for questions 1, 3 and 10 are given on pages 63–65.

Exam questions

Planning an essay

There are several ways of planning an essay either for coursework or as part of an examination. One of the quickest, simplest and easiest to follow is the spidergram. Creating a spidergram is easy, just complete the following steps.

- Put the key words of the essay question in the centre of your map and work outwards from this.

- Make sure you use different colours if the essay asks you to look at either different characters or different themes. This will make them easy to isolate at a glance.

- Draw lines out from the centre that relate directly to the question. From these lines, draw further lines and write anything specifically related to this area of the question.

- Remember, only have one idea at the end of each line or your drawing may become confusing.

- The next few pages show you how you could use spidergrams to plan the answers to three of the sample essay questions.

If you find that using spidergrams is not for you, don't panic, there are other ways of planning your answers.

- You can underline the key words in the title to ensure that you understand the focus of the essay.

- Then use bullet points to write down what will be included in each paragraph, from the introduction to the conclusion.

- Next, try to find relevant quotations to support your points and either write down the quotation or page reference so that it can be found easily.

- Ensure that you stick to your plan and refer back to the question so as not to digress from it.

- In an examination, always hand in any plan that you have written as you may be given some credit for it if you are unable to complete the full essay.

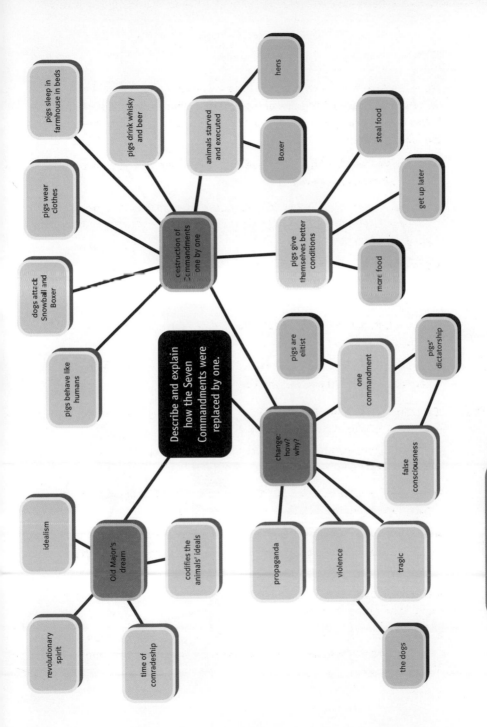

Describe and explain how the Seven Commandments were replaced by one.

- destruction of commandments one by one
  - pigs sleep in farmhouse in beds
  - pigs drink whisky and beer
  - animals starved and executed
    - hens
    - Boxer
  - pigs wear clothes
  - dogs attack Snowball and Boxer
  - pigs behave like humans
  - pigs give themselves better conditions
    - steal food
    - get up later
    - more food

- change: how? why?
  - pigs are elitist
  - one commandment
    - pigs' dictatorship
  - false consciousness
  - propaganda
  - violence
  - tragic
  - the dogs

- Old Major's dream
  - idealism
  - codifies the animals' ideals
  - revolutionary spirit
  - time of comradeship

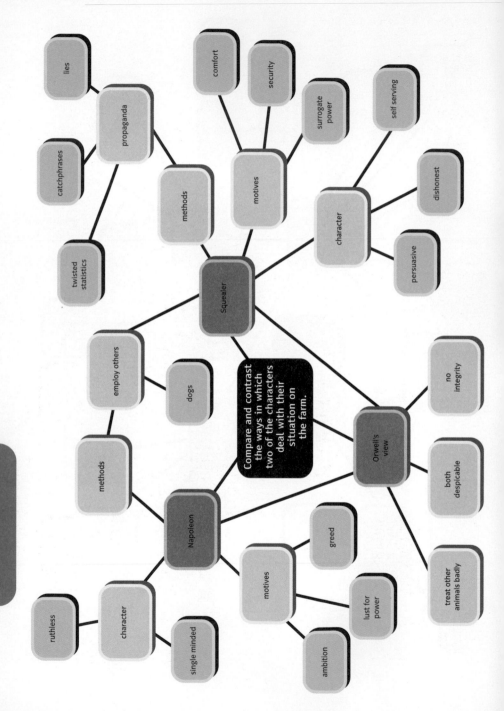

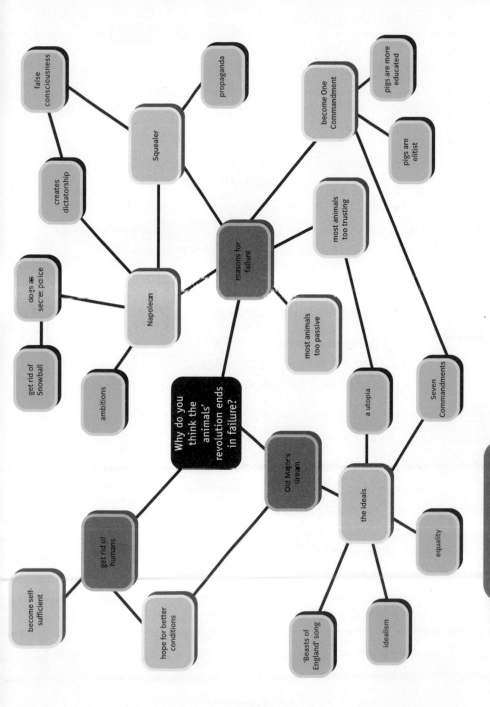

Why do you think the animals' revolution ends in failure?

- false consciousness
- propaganda
- Squealer
- creates dictatorship
- become One Commandment
    - pigs are more educated
    - pigs are elitist
- reasons for failure
- most animals too trusting
- Napoleon
    - acts as secret police
    - get rid of Snowball
    - ambitions
- most animals too passive
- a utopia
- Seven Commandments
- Old Major's dream
- the ideals
    - equality
    - idealism
    - 'Beasts of England' song
- get rid of humans
    - become self-sufficient
    - hope for better conditions

Spidergram essay plans

65

Sample response

Why do you think the animals' revolution ends in failure?

There are a number of reasons why the animals' revolution ends in failure by the end of 'Animal Farm'. These include the selfish nature of the pigs, Napoleon's ambition to be the only one in charge, the animals' lack of realisation that they are being oppressed until it is too late and the use of propaganda to convince the animals of the version of events those in charge want them to believe. ✔ Each of these contributes to the eventual failure of the revolution that was born from the ideal that animals could live in a state of equality away from slavery by man, and that because of this all their lives would be improved. ✔

Old Major's dream ✔ is where the ideas for the revolution begin. He tells of a world where all animals unite to overthrow man and to work for better lives for themselves. He explains:

'Whatever goes upon two legs, is an enemy. Whatever goes upon four legs, or has wings, is a friend.'

He urges the animals to remember this but dies before the revolution begins and is replaced by Snowball and Napoleon, who together become the leaders and take over the farm. They have different skills. Snowball is a good speaker and is brave and wants to carry on Old Major's ideals. Napoleon is quieter but believed to be a deeper character and thus soon they are disagreeing on how to run the farm. ✔ Snowball becomes obsessed with the windmill project and does not realise Napoleon is plotting to overthrow him. ✔ He recognises the importance of the animals learning to read and write and tries his best to teach them. Napoleon would prefer they remained ignorant and therefore easier to manipulate. ✔

The ability or lack of it to communicate becomes very important on the farm. ✔ It is the inability of the animals to read or understand what is going on that contributes to the failure of their revolution. Snowball reads the Seven Commandments to the animals, but some do not understand them and so they are simplified down to 'FOUR LEGS GOOD, TWO LEGS BAD'. This does not compensate for the pigs being more educated, which through the course of the novel gives them power. When the animals question anything, their inability to read is held against them. Boxer refuses to believe that Snowball was in league with Jones and says that Snowball was shot by Jones. Squealer claims that Snowball confessed this in writing. ✔

'Jones's shot only grazed him. I could show you this in his own writing, if you were able to read it.'

This comment is intended to make Boxer feel inferior and deter him from questioning Squealer further. When the Seven Commandments are altered, the animals are led to believe that they have not remembered them accurately. ✔

Napoleon remains in power by recruiting animals with certain skills to be loyal to him. One such animal is a porker called Squealer, who is a good speaker with a persuasive manner. Napoleon is not a good orator so Squealer becomes his 'propaganda machine'. ✔ He lies to the animals and rewrites certain events that have taken place to suit what Napoleon wants them to believe. The animals' willingness to believe everything they are told and not realising that they are being manipulated, contributes to the failure of the revolution. ✔

Once the animals believe in Napoleon as their leader, he maintains his rule through fear. ✔ He uses the dogs as a kind of secret police who are willing to kill anyone who questions his rule. It is they who chase Snowball off the farm and they who make sure no one helps the hens when they rebel. By the time the animals realise what is happening it is too late and Napoleon is too strong to be got rid of. ✔ His supporters like the lifestyle he offers them and are determined to keep it no matter what. Eventually Napoleon shows his true colours, but by then it is too late. ✔ Orwell says:

'out came Napoleon himself, majestically upright, casting haughty glances from side to side, and with his dogs gambolling round him. He carried a whip in his trotter.'

This shows how he is definitely not one of them any more. He is carrying a weapon to make them work harder and is willing to hurt them if they do not.

In conclusion, the reasons the revolution ends in failure is a mixture of the greed of the pigs, Napoleon's ambition to be leader and the animals not realising what is going on until it is too late to do anything about it. ✔ He is able to rule by fear and manages to get enough supporters to make sure he cannot be got rid of.

By the end of the novel all the ideas of Old Major are nothing more than a dream. ✓

> ## Examiner's comments
>
> *This essay demonstrates some understanding of what caused the revolution to fail but is not sufficiently analytical. The candidate needs to highlight that all the animals are to some extent to blame and that Old Major was unaware that his teachings could be deliberately misinterpreted by those with ambition. The conclusion is not really sufficient in summing up the main points of the essay and could answer the original question more clearly*

Sample response

Why do you think the animals' revolution ends in failure?

'Animalism', the revolutionary doctrine adopted by the animals is based on the ideas of Old Major and is translated into the Seven Commandments, a document which Orwell based on the ideas of the Communist Manifesto. ✓ Ironically, these ideas stem from Old Major's dream of a world where animals would unite, overthrow humans and live worthwhile lives in a Utopia. Sadly, by the end of the novel that is all it is — a dream. ✓ There are a number of reasons for this and a number of animals to whom blame can be attributed, both those who lead the rebellion and those who follow. 'Animal Farm' is an allegory of the Russian Revolution and mirrors the reasons it failed. ✓

Old Major's ideas offer an alternative for the animals to their lives under the rule of Mr and Mrs Jones. ✓ Old Major is adamant that there is a better existence available to the animals away from the tyranny of man, and that in order to achieve this all animals must become united. ✓ He explains:

'And among us animals let there be perfect unity, perfect comradeship in the struggle. All men are enemies. All animals are comrades.'

This demonstrates his understanding that the only way there is any chance of success is for all animals to unite and rebel against the oppression under which they currently live. ✓ He asks animals to set aside their disputes with other animals to achieve a greater good. Unfortunately, Old Major does not consider the notion that his teachings might be used for individual animals to fulfil their own greedy ambitions at the expense of others. ✔ He also fails to consider that such ideals are open to a number of different interpretations. His death before the rebellion means that it is not he that will ultimately lead the animals. ✔

One of the leaders, Snowball, clearly prioritises the importance of educating the animals. The pigs have taught themselves to read and write and Snowball actively encourages all animals to attain literacy skills. ✔ However, a number of the animals have neither the intelligence nor the inclination to learn, and this is the first step away from the ideal of the Utopia. When the Seven Commandments are written, it is the fact that some of the animals cannot read them, understand them properly or in time remember them that make it so easy to alter them without the animals realising. ✔ The Commandments codify the ideals of the animals and their comradeship. The alteration of these by the pigs as and when it suits them and the blind acceptance of this by the other animals, shows that those who are more educated are automatically empowered. ✔ Napoleon and the other pigs are aware of this and use it to their advantage, but Snowball to his credit attempts to simplify the Commandments to one sentence: 'FOUR LEGS GOOD, TWO LEGS BAD'. This is unfortunately not sufficient to prevent the animals' memories from being manipulated and certain events on the farm from, in time, being rewritten. ✔ After Napoleon expels Snowball from the farm and gains sole leadership of the newly named 'Animal Farm', Snowball is used as a scapegoat when anything goes wrong. Squealer explains:

'Snowball has sold himself to Frederick of Pinchfield Farm, who is now plotting to attack us and take our farm away from us!'

This makes the animals believe that Napoleon is a better leader, who protects them from the threat of Snowball who was destroying their ideals from within. ✔ In actual fact it is Napoleon who is self-serving and wants to 'brainwash' the animals into compliance.

Squealer is the means by which Napoleon convinces the animals that their lives are better under his rule. ✔ The animals are lured into false consciousness and believe that they are working as equals when from the beginning all the pigs do is oversee the hard work and issue orders. Squealer's job is to spread propaganda and to stifle the animals' understanding or awareness of real events. ✔ He is extremely important to Napoleon as an instrument with which to misinform the animals in the most convincing way. Squealer, like Snowball, is an accomplished orator and has a very convincing manner. Napoleon does not possess this skill and therefore ensures that Squealer shows him total loyalty by offering him a life of luxury. Squealer will not risk this as he wants to remain one of the privileged few. ✔ Unlike Snowball he is motivated by his own desires for a comfortable life and is the equivalent of the vast media machines that present the government version of events in any dictatorship. ✓ He constantly uses the threat that Jones might return when any animal questions decisions made. The animals' willingness to believe his lies and half-truths certainly contribute to the failure of the revolution as the animals cease to question anything the pigs say and do. When Boxer questions Squealer's assertion that Snowball was in league with Jones from the beginning, Squealer explains that Napoleon has decreed it to be so and Boxer immediately believes him. ✓ Unfortunately, Squealer now perceives Boxer as a threat to the security of the pigs' power. Orwell describes how

'it was noticed that he cast a very ugly look at Boxer with his twinkling little eyes.'

It becomes increasingly apparent that after this incident it is only a matter of time until Squealer will rid the farm of Boxer, as any risk to the survival of the regime must be dealt with. Boxer is also partially responsible for the failure of the revolution as he is unquestioningly loyal to Napoleon and naively believes that every animal's intentions are as noble as his own. ✓ The animals' failure to question the pigs' rule early enough is one of the major reasons the revolution fails. ✓

From the beginning, while Snowball is obsessed with the windmill project, Napoleon is amassing a group of loyal supporters such as Squealer, Minimus and the dogs. He takes the dogs from their mothers shortly after they are born and trains them to be his 'secret police'. It is they who chase Snowball from the farm, they who execute animals as an example to others and they who ensure that the other animals do not feed the hens when they rebel, and are willing to kill anyone who violates this order. They are unquestioningly loyal to Napoleon, and by the time that some of the animals realise that the pigs are oppressors not comrades, it is too late, Napoleon cannot be deposed. The farm has become a dictatorship but the animals are powerless to do anything about it. ✓

Benjamin, the oldest animal on the farm only chooses to air the cynical views he has felt from the start when he realises that Boxer is being sent to the knacker's yard. Throughout the novel, there have been incidents where Benjamin could have confided his misgivings about their situation to others, but he chooses not to. As he reads the outside of the van Boxer is in and watches the illiterate ignorant animals waving to Boxer, he finally finds his voice: ✓

'Do you not understand what that means? They are taking Boxer to the knacker's.'

It is too late and nothing can be done. Most of the animals have either been indoctrinated into thinking the way the pigs want them to, like the sheep, or are too afraid to do anything. Had Benjamin spoken up sooner, as a well-respected animal on the farm he may have been able to alter the course of events. ✓

Ultimately, there are a number of reasons for the failure of the revolution. The pigs are immediately not equal to the other animals as they have learnt to read and write, which automatically places them at an advantage. They are able to manipulate the written word so that the other animals, unsure whether alterations have been made or not, become confused and distrust their own memories. One by one the pigs break the Commandments and alter them to benefit themselves, and gradually this corruption leads to the destruction of all their original ideals. ✓ In addition to this there is the blind loyalty of characters such as Boxer to the leader and the supposed ideals of what they are trying to achieve. But Boxer is simply an example: the animals' unwillingness, or in some cases inability, to think for themselves makes them easy to manipulate. They allow themselves to be lured into a state of false consciousness where they believe that their lives are better under this new regime and are convinced by propaganda and the dictator's rewriting of history. ✓ At the point where some of them realise that their conditions are far from ideal, Napoleon and his followers start to rule by fear and have too much power to usurp. The animals' revolution is a failure because of the greed and ambition of some animals and the inability of other animals to recognise this quality in others. The pigs become elitist and no challenge is made to this until it is too late, by which time the animals are already living in a worse regime than before. Their revolution and ideals are a thing of the past, a dream, and they are once more living in a nightmare where 'ALL ANIMALS ARE EQUAL, BUT SOME ANIMALS ARE MORE EQUAL THAN OTHERS.' ✓

Examiner's comments

This essay shows a good knowledge of why the revolution failed. The candidate has effectively analysed the events, as well as discussing how certain animals can have blame attributed to them. There could have been closer examination of how Squealer uses language to convince the animals, and the contrast between his methods of persuasion and Old Major's. The essay would also have benefited from an examination of the role Moses has to play as a representative of organised religion.

Quick quiz 1
Uncover the plot
Mr Jones goes to bed drunk and the animals all gather in the big barn to hear Old Major speak. The pig tells of the misery Man causes animals and preaches rebellion; finally he relates his dream of a golden future in a song: 'Beasts of England'.

Old Major dies, and the animals continue to hold secret meetings organised by the pigs, the most intelligent animals. The rebellion is spontaneous; Jones gets drunk again and forgets to feed the animals, so they drive him, his wife and his men off the farm. They burn all the reins, bits, whips and knives, and enter the farmhouse with fear.

Snowball changes the name of the farm on the gate and writes up the Seven Commandments. The hay harvest is the best ever and all summer the animals are happy. On Sundays there is no work and their flag is hoisted — a white horn and hoof on a green background. Snowball sums up the Commandments as: 'Four legs good, two legs bad', which the sheep repeat endlessly.

Snowball and Napoleon disagree about everything. Napoleon takes nine puppies away to educate them secretly. Apples and milk are reserved for the pigs.

Quick quiz 2
Uncover the plot
The fame of Animal Farm grows and, in particular, its <u>song</u>*. In* <u>October</u>*, the* <u>pigeons</u> *bring news that Jones is leading an attack. He is defeated with only* <u>one</u> *animal killed. Snowball and* <u>Boxer</u> *are given medals for bravery.*

<u>Mollie</u> is the first animal to desert the farm. The frequent disagreements between Snowball and <u>Napoleon</u> reach a climax over the construction of the <u>windmill</u>. The animals are swept away by <u>Snowball's</u> eloquent pleading, but are prevented from voting for him by Napoleon's dogs who <u>chase him away</u>. Napoleon assumes power and abolishes <u>debates</u>.

<u>Three</u> weeks later, he announces that the windmill will be built after all, over <u>two</u> years. <u>Boxer</u> works the hardest in this task. <u>Mr Whymper</u> is appointed to act as an intermediary in trading with humans. In <u>November</u>, a storm destroys the windmill and building begins again. Food is scarce and <u>eggs are</u> sold to acquire it; meanwhile, Snowball is blamed for everything that goes wrong.

Quick quiz 3
Uncover the plot
Napoleon continues to become less <u>accessible</u>. He plays <u>Pilkington</u> and Frederick against each other over the proposed sale of <u>timber</u>, and is <u>enraged</u> when he discovers he has been tricked.

<u>Frederick</u> attacks the farm and destroys the windmill with <u>gunpowder</u>. Six animals are killed but the humans are defeated. To celebrate, the pigs drink <u>whisky</u>. <u>Boxer</u> has injured his hoof but is due to retire on this <u>12th</u> birthday. Rations are <u>reduced</u> and Animal Farm becomes a <u>Republic</u>.

<u>Boxer</u> collapses and is sold to the slaughterhouse by the <u>pigs</u>, who hold a <u>banquet</u> in his honour.

<u>Years pass</u> and the farm grows <u>richer</u>. <u>Few</u> of the animals remember life before the rebellion and they still have <u>pride</u> in their farm. This is destroyed when the pigs begin to <u>walk on their hind legs</u>. Only one of the Commandments remains and in the final scene, pigs and humans are shown <u>at a party</u>. Animal Farm is now to be called <u>Manor Farm</u>. When the pigs and men start to <u>argue</u> together, they become indistinguishable from each other.

Good luck with your GCSEs!

Page 14, George Orwell, © Corbis Sygma
Page 17, Scene, © Popperfoto/Alamy.com

Page 60 questions 1–3. Examination questions reproduced by kind permission of the Assessment and Qualifications Alliance. The answers supplied to the Exam Board questions are solely the responsibility of the authors, and are not supplied or approved by the Exam Boards.

The author and publishers are grateful to the Estate of Sonia Bronwell Orwell for permission to quote from *Animal Farm* by George Orwell, published by Secker and Warburg Ltd.

First published 1994
Revised edition 2004

Letts Educational
Chiswick Centre
414 Chiswick High Road
London W4 5TF
Tel: 020 8996 3333

Cover and text design by Hardlines Ltd., Charlbury, Oxfordshire.

Typeset by Letterpart Ltd., Reigate, Surrey.

Graphic illustration by Beehive Illustration, Cirencester, Gloucestershire.

Commissioned by Cassandra Birmingham

Editorial project management by Vicky Butt

Printed in Italy.

British Library Cataloguing in Publication Data. A CIP record of this book is available from the British Library.

ISBN 1 84315 317 3

Letts Educational is a division of Granada Learning, part of Granada plc.